GRADES 1-3
Ages 6-10

Erica Nolan

Print Handwriting
Workbook for Kids

Fun Activities, Letters, Numbers, Sight Words

Improve, Learn and Engage!

ZEFIRS PUBLISHING

Dear Caregiver,

Handwriting practice is an exciting journey—it's a crucial skill for your child's development in today's digital age. Thank you for choosing this book and supporting your child's development with us.

Learning to trace and write letters enhances cognitive development, memory, and academic performance while improving attention to detail, reading, and language skills—essential for your child's success.

Our handwriting practice book transforms learning into an enjoyable adventure. Inside, children will discover puzzles, tracing activities, and illustrations designed to keep them engaged and motivated at their own pace.

To celebrate your child's hard work and dedication, we've included a special certificate at the end of this book. Once they complete all activities, cut it out and award it along with a special treat—a token of their success and progress.

Contents

Welcome, little writer!
A few tips before you start:

① Maintain good posture. Sit up straight with your feet flat on the floor to improve your writing comfort and efficiency.

② Pick the right pencil. Softer B pencils glide smoothly on paper. Once you've mastered the letters, try using an ink pen.

③ Mind your grip. Ensure the pad of your thumb touches the pencil for easy, fluid writing motions.

④ Be patient! Improving your handwriting is a journey. Remember, great things take time.

⑤ Take breaks. Short breaks help keep your hand relaxed and your mind fresh.

This is me

My name is

....

My favourite

Food: ....

Color: ....

Animal: ....

Sport: ....

Place: ....

Music: ....

My birthday is

....

I am .... years old

I want to go to

....

I like

....

....

I don't like

....

My best friend is

....

Before starting the book, write down this sentence. Once you've finished, rewrite it and see how much your handwriting has improved.

Write: A happy unicorn jumps over the lazy dog and finds a box of mixed jewels.

BEFORE

Date: . . . .

AFTER

Date: . . . .

PART 1
Letters

A chameleon's tongue is twice the length of its body.

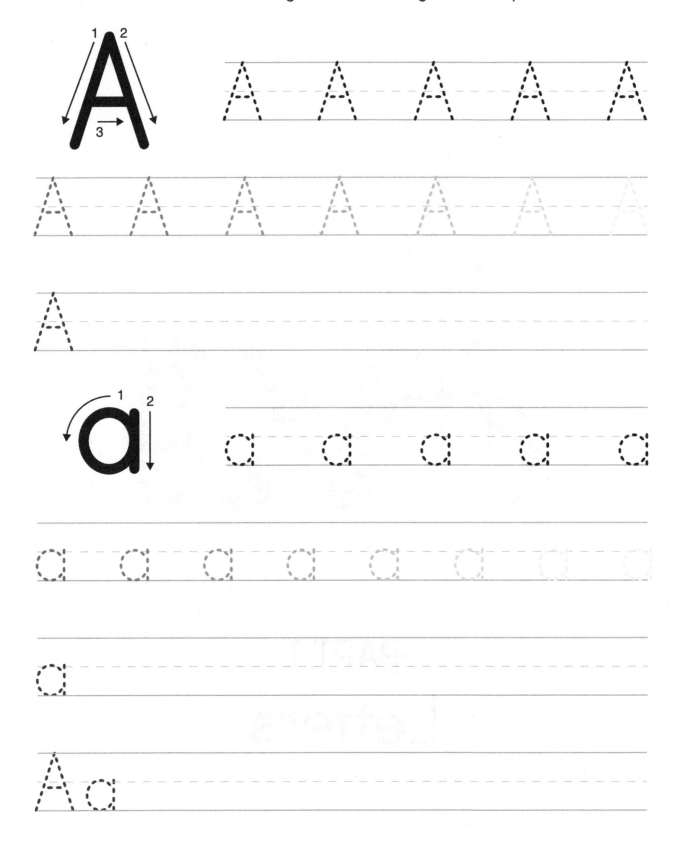

Draw an apple!

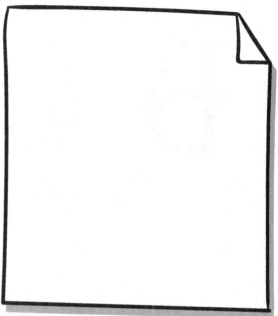

Trace the sentence:

After every dance
class, Amelia the
alligator enjoys a
crisp apple.

Giraffes can clean their ears with their tongues.

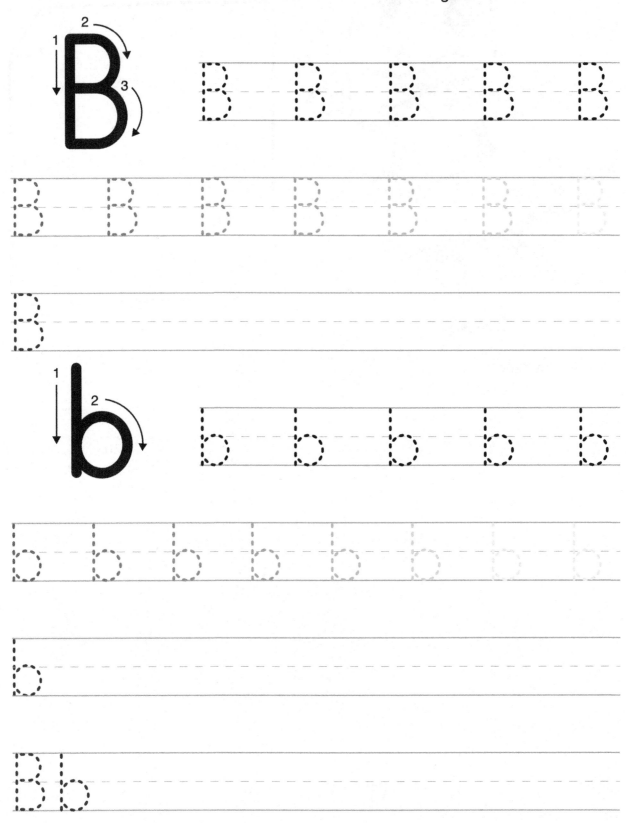

Trace the lines, add some sprinkles, and color the image!

Trace the sentence:

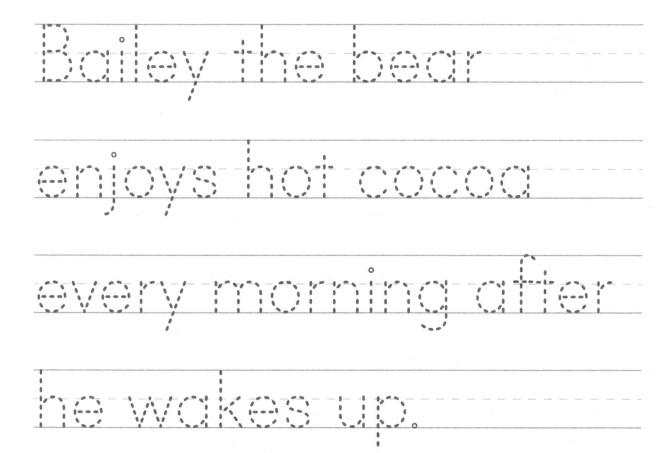

Bailey the bear

enjoys hot cocoa

every morning after

he wakes up.

Elephants are the only mammals that can't jump.

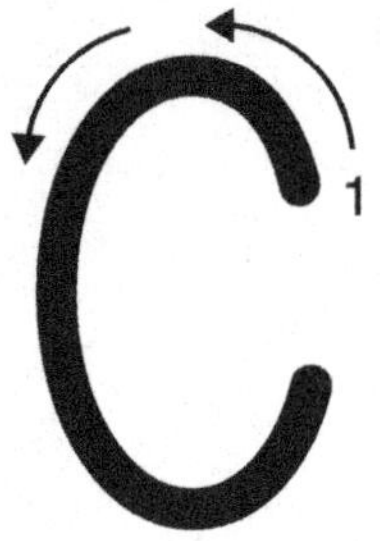

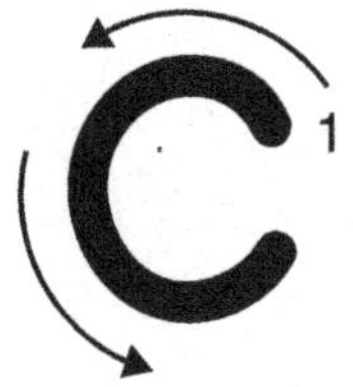

C   C C C C C

C C C C C C C

C

C C C C C

C C C C C C C

C

Cc

Guide Colin through the maze!

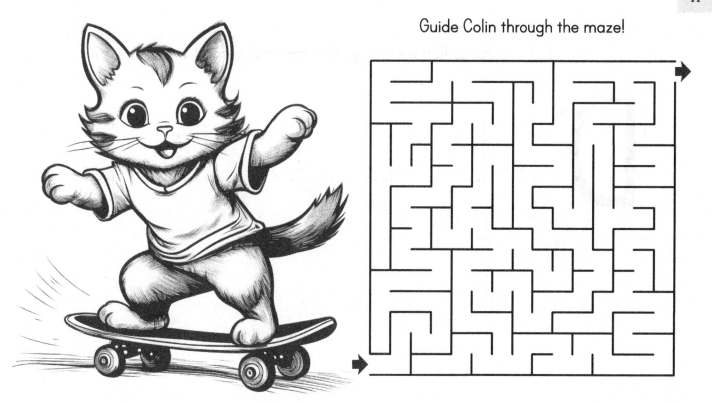

Trace the sentence:

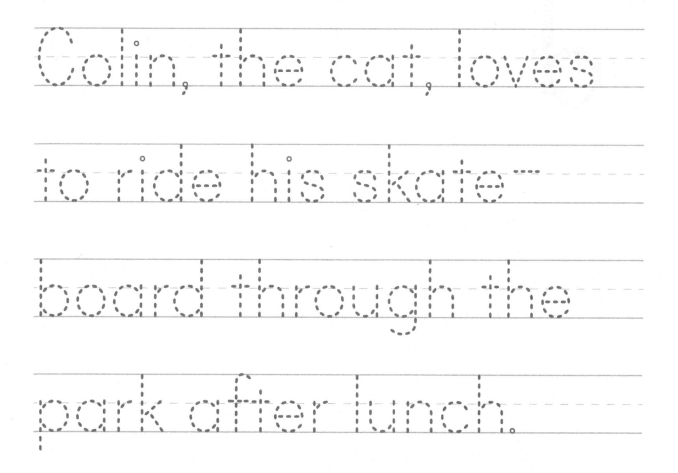

Colin, the cat, loves
to ride his skate
board through the
park after lunch.

Hummingbirds flap their wings 80 times per second.

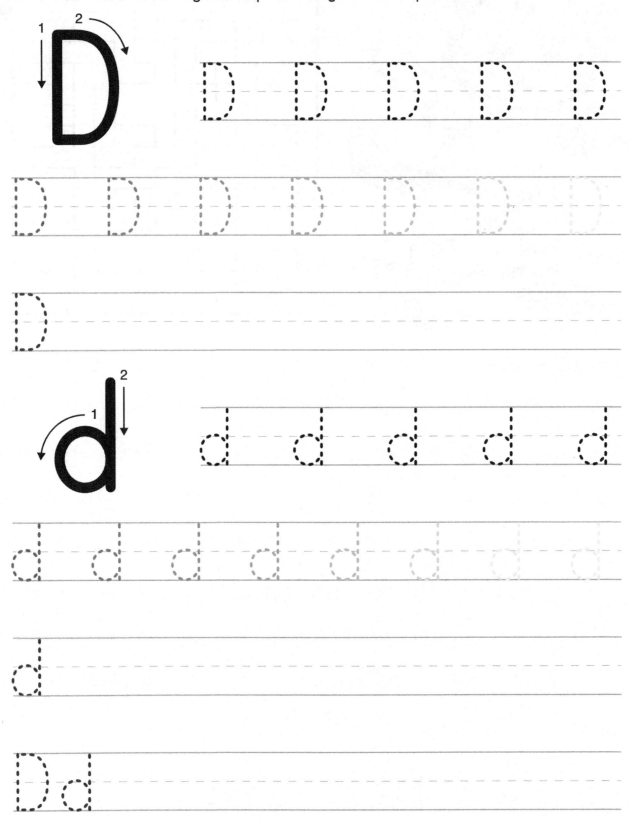

Finish the picture and color it in!

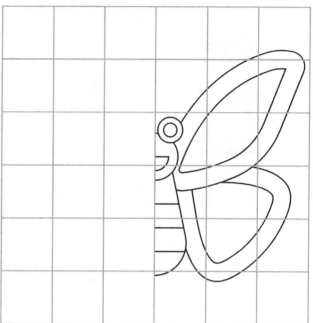

Trace the sentence:

Duke the dog loves
chasing butterflies,
running through
the garden.

A group of owls is called a parliament.

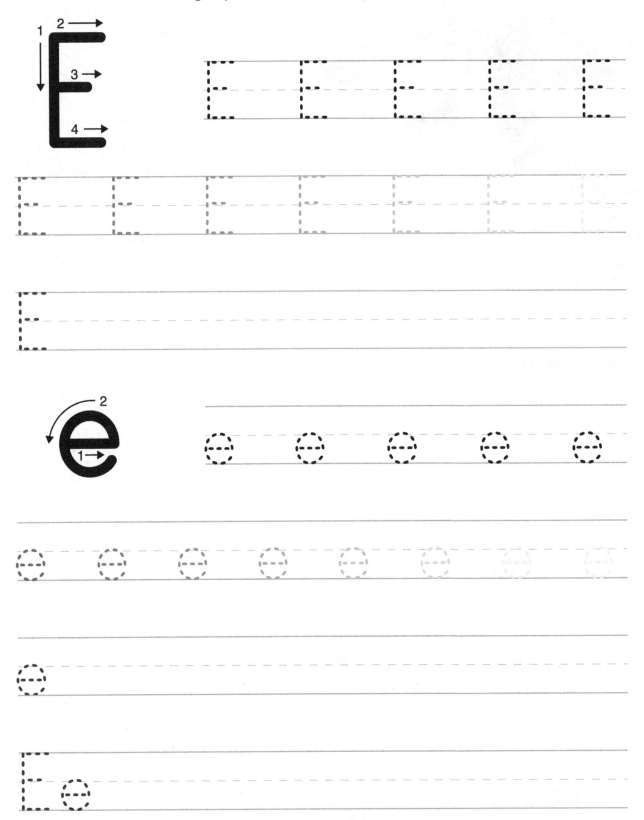

Ha! Ha! Ha! Ha!

Q: What would you do if an elephant sat in front of you at a movie?
A: Miss most of the film.

Q: What time is it when an elephant sits on the fence?
A: Time to fix the fence!

Q: Why did the elephant flap its ears?
A: Because it was its biggest fan.

Trace the sentence:

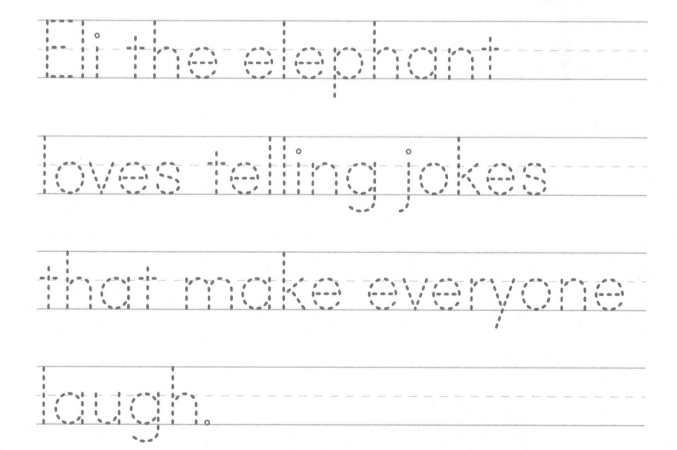

Eli the elephant loves telling jokes that make everyone laugh.

A shrimp's heart is in its head.

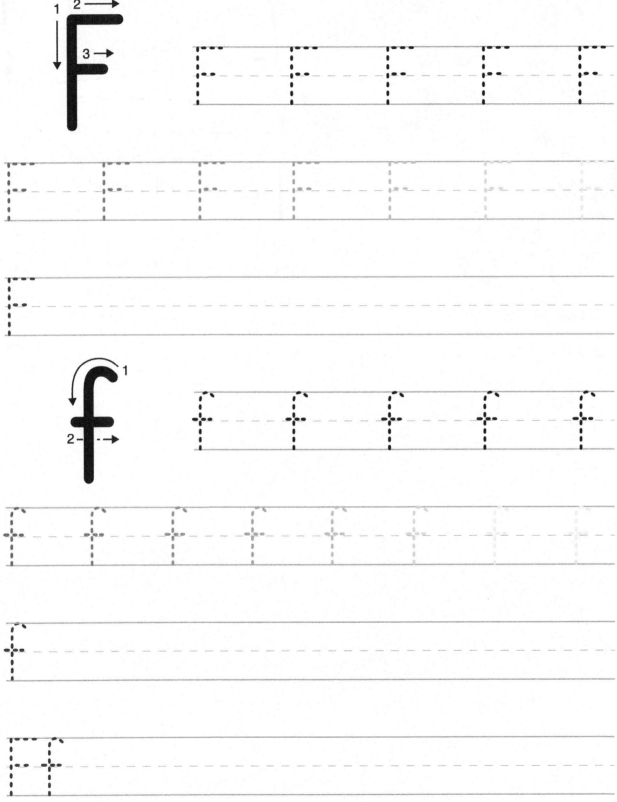

Fred the frog is feeling down. Draw or write what could cheer him up.

Trace the sentence:

Fred the frog had a bad day. His lily pad drifted off and vanished.

Some lizards can regrow their tails.

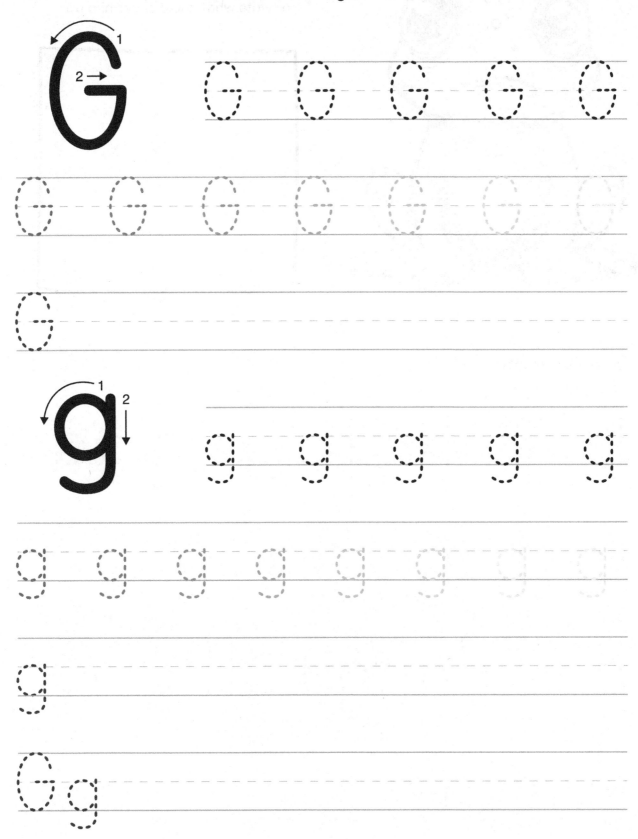

Trace the sentence:

Gus the goat

enjoys playing

guitar by the barn,

strumming all day.

Octopuses can squeeze through tiny spaces.

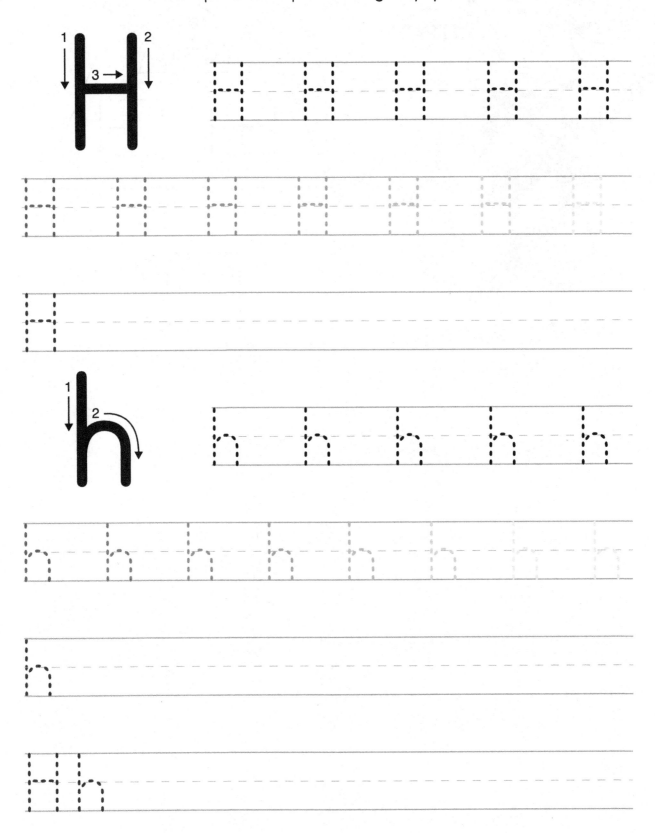

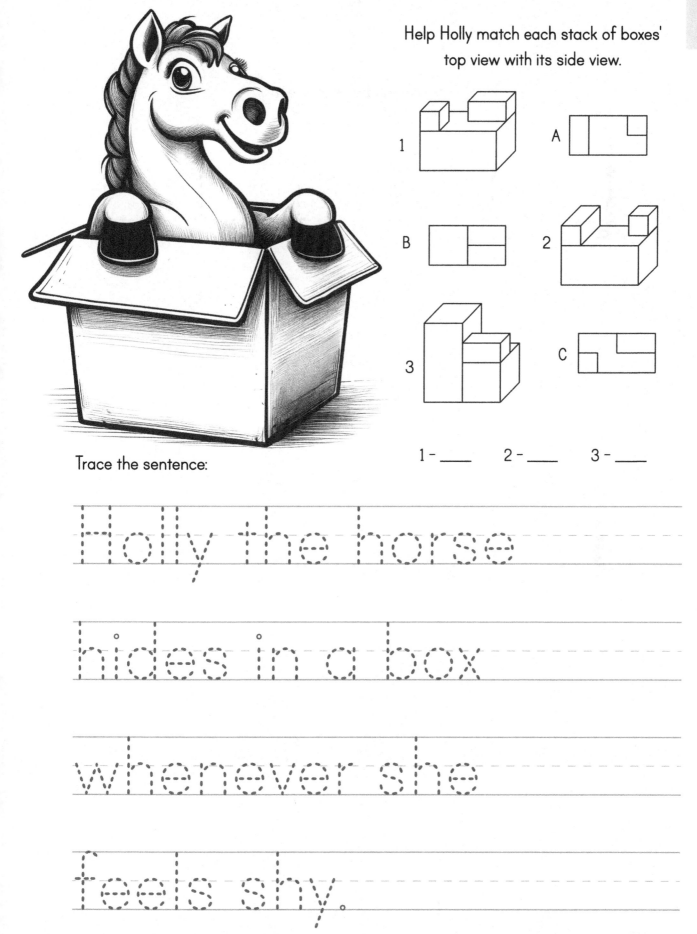

Help Holly match each stack of boxes' top view with its side view.

1

A

B

2

3

C

1 - ___   2 - ___   3 - ___

Trace the sentence:

Holly the horse

hides in a box

whenever she

feels shy.

Elephants use mud as sunscreen.

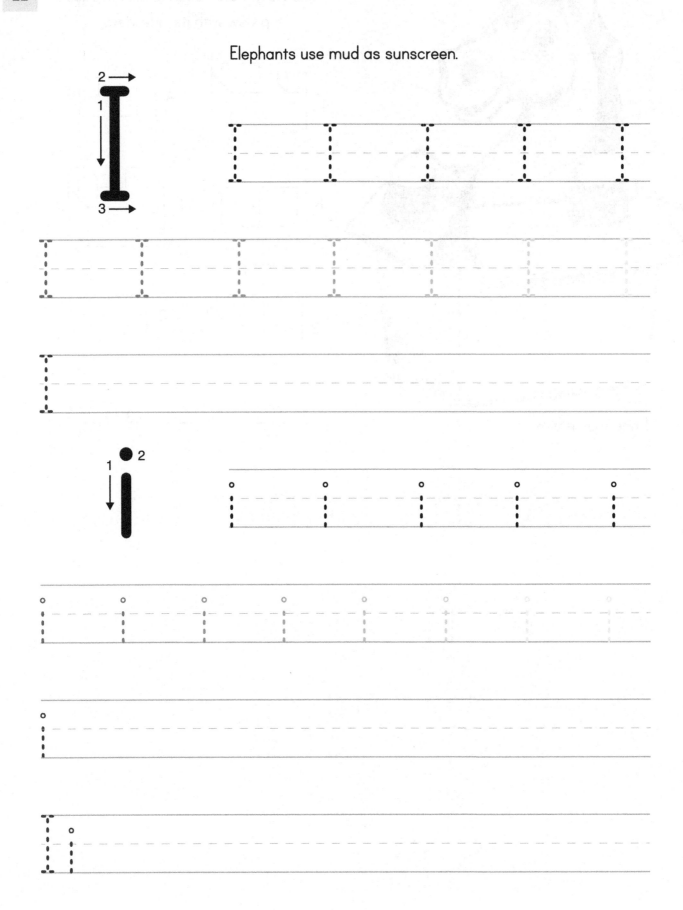

DID YOU KNOW?

Iguanas are the **largest lizards** native to South and Central America.

Iguanas are great **climbers** and frequently perch in trees. They're also strong **swimmers**, using their tails to help them move through the water.

Iguanas usually choose to run away but can protect themselves with their tail, claws, and teeth. If their **tail** is lost while escaping a predator, it will **grow back**.

Trace the sentence:

Izzy the iguana loves swimming in the cool river on hot sunny days.

Hummingbirds are the only birds that can fly backward.

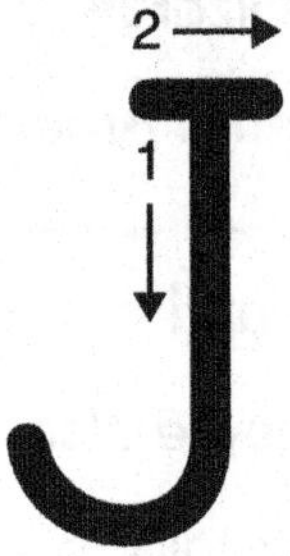

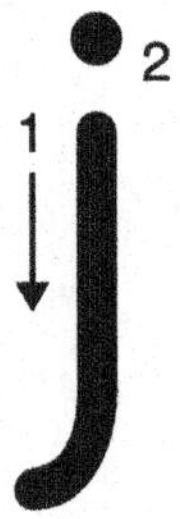

J

J J J J J

J J J J J J

J

j

j j j j j

j j j j j j j j

j

J j

Fill in the blanks by drawing
the missing sea creatures.

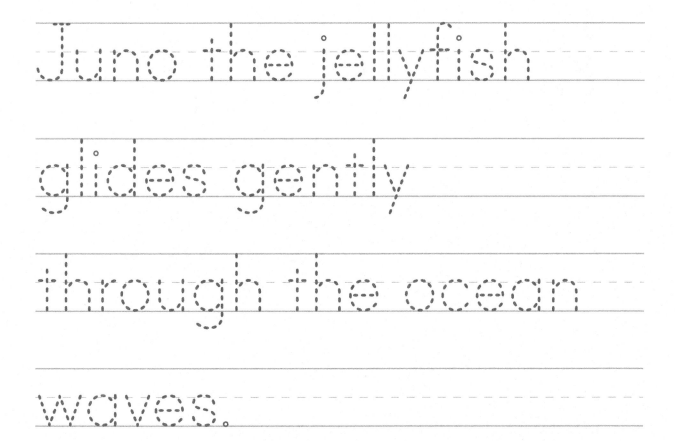

Trace the sentence:

Juno the jellyfish

glides gently

through the ocean

waves.

Bats are the only mammals that can fly.

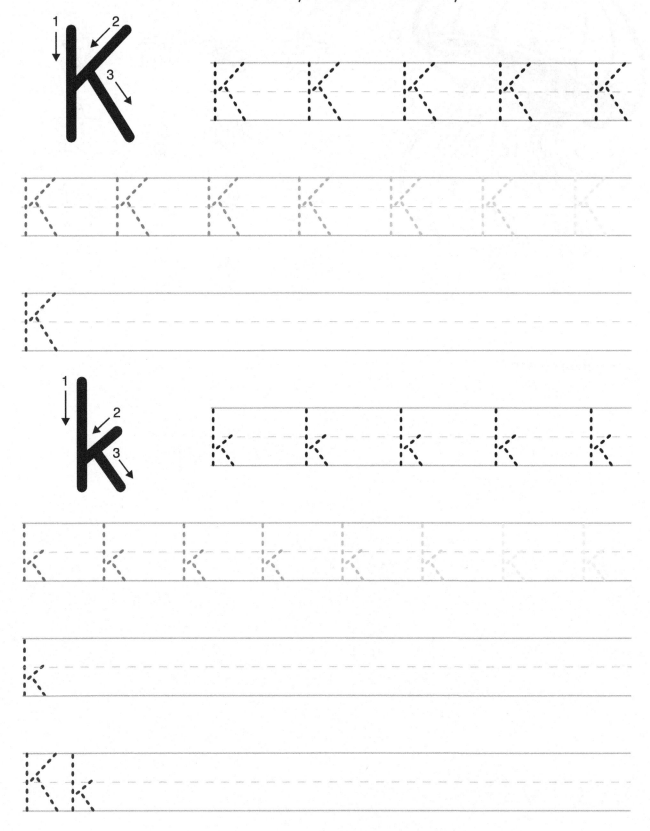

Can you count how many "K's" are in the picture?

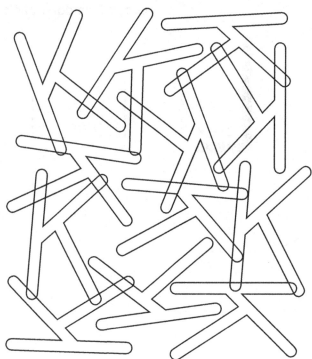

Trace the sentence:

Kate the kangaroo

teaches her baby

letters, showing

them one by one.

Crocodiles can't stick their tongues out.

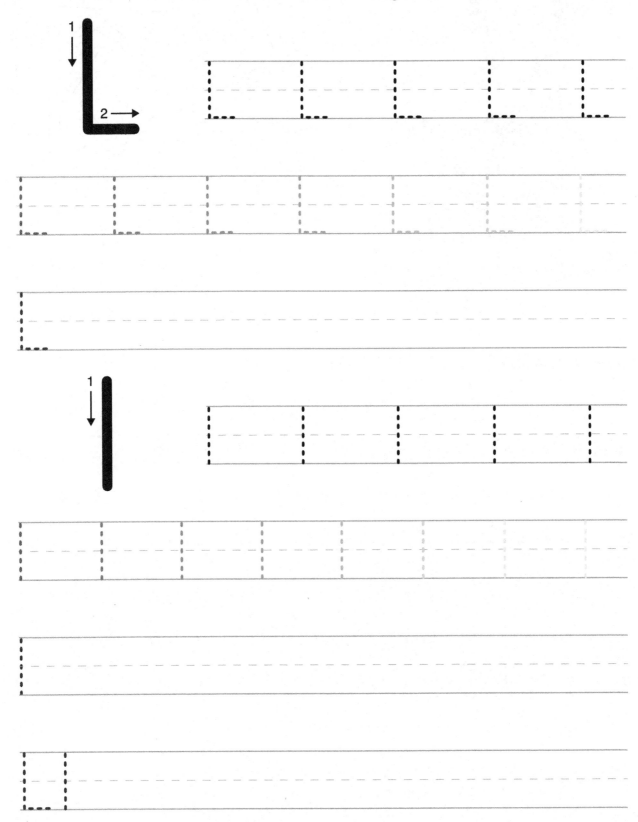

Can you figure out Leo's favorite TV show? Use the clues below to decode and solve the puzzle!

8	6	11	8	1	7	3

9	1	2	4

2	4	10

5	2	11	8	5

1 = I   2 = T   3 = G   4 = H   5 = S   6 = O
7 = N   8 = R   9 = W   10 = E   11 = A

Trace the sentence:

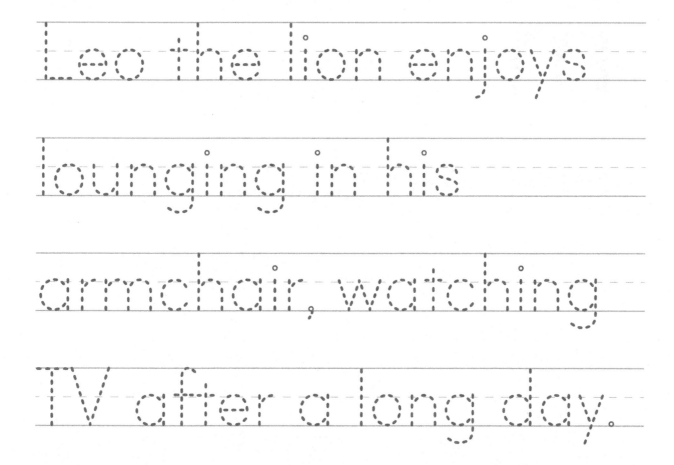

Leo the lion enjoys lounging in his armchair, watching TV after a long day.

Zebras' stripes are unique like fingerprints.

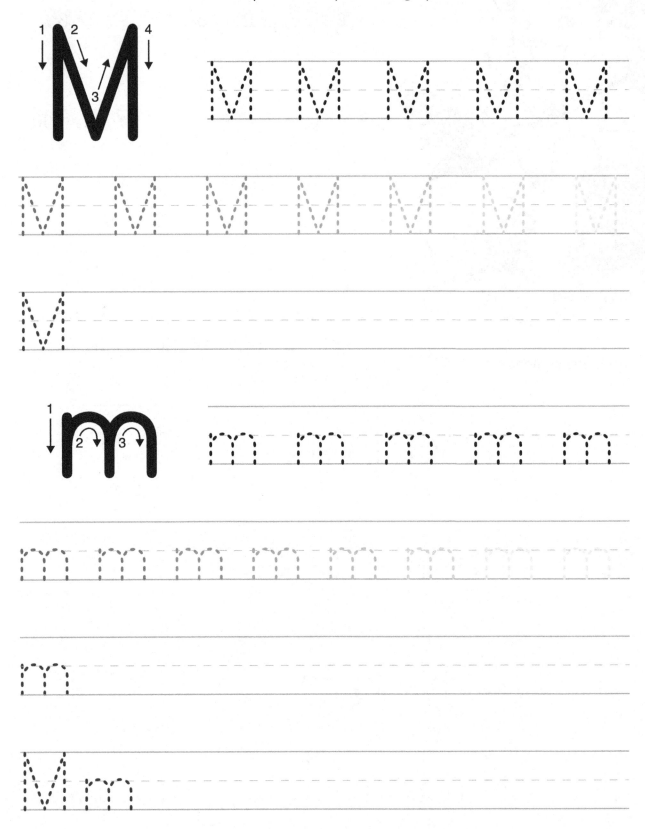

Ha! Ha! Ha!

Q: Why are mice scared of swimming in the water?
A: Because of all the catfish in it!

Q: What do mice eat on their birthdays?
A: Cheesecake.

Q: What do mice say to each other when they meet for the very first time?
A: It is so mice to meet you!

Trace the sentence:

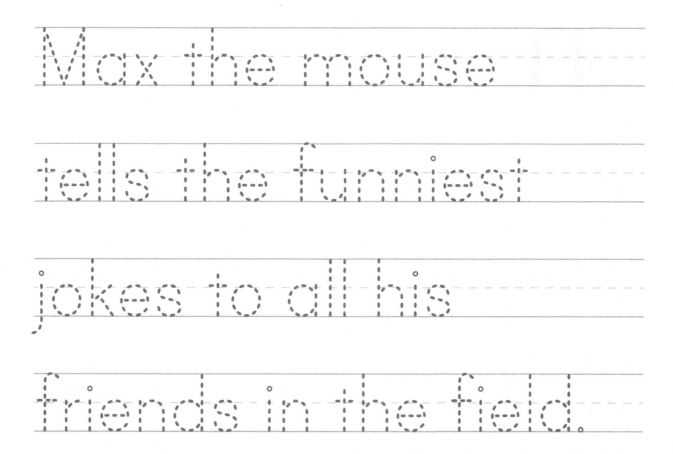

Max the mouse tells the funniest jokes to all his friends in the field.

Sharks have been around for 400 million years.

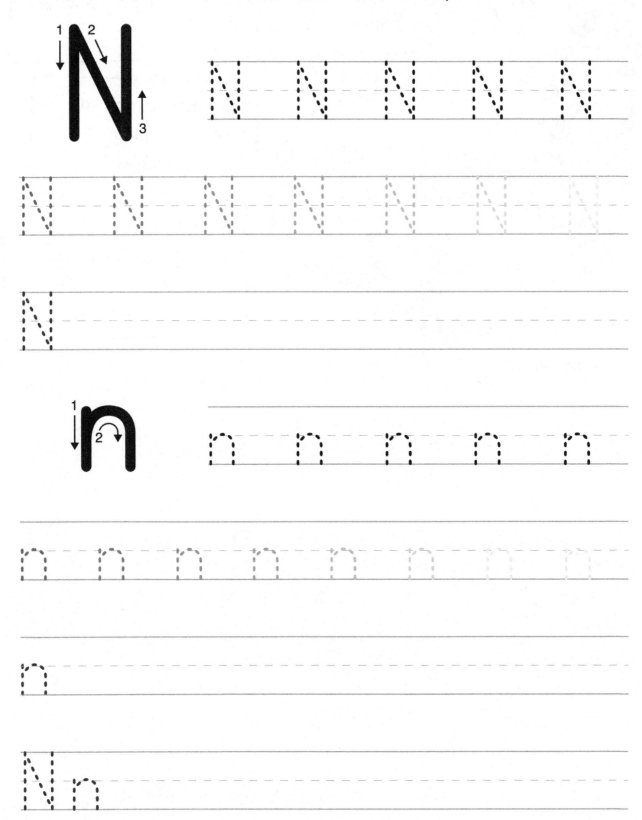

DID YOU KNOW?

Nutrias are large, semi-aquatic rodents often **mistaken for beavers**. However, they can easily be distinguished by their tails.

They have **bright orange teeth** that are super strong and help them chew through tough plants.

Nutrias love to snack on roots and aquatic plants, but they also enjoy munching on fruits and vegetables, **eating up to 25% of their body weight** daily!

Trace the sentence:

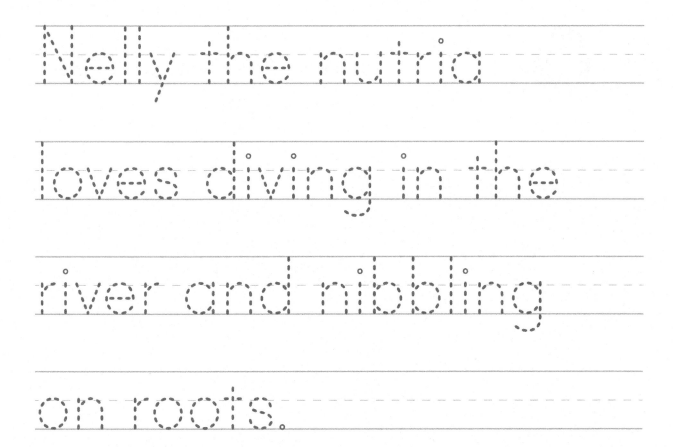

Nelly the nutria loves diving in the river and nibbling on roots.

Only female mosquitoes bite.

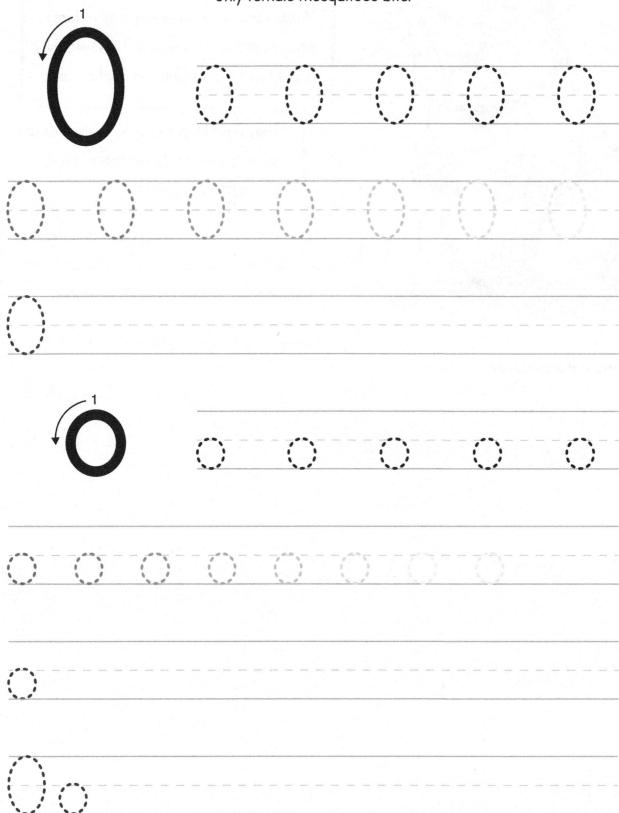

Trace the lines and color the image!

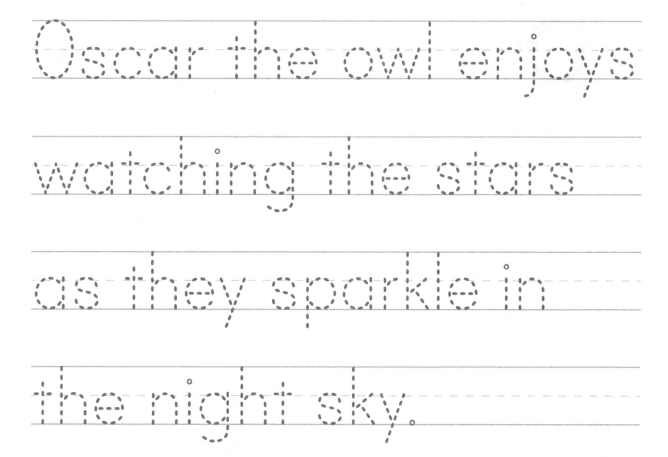

Trace the sentence:

Oscar the owl enjoys
watching the stars
as they sparkle in
the night sky.

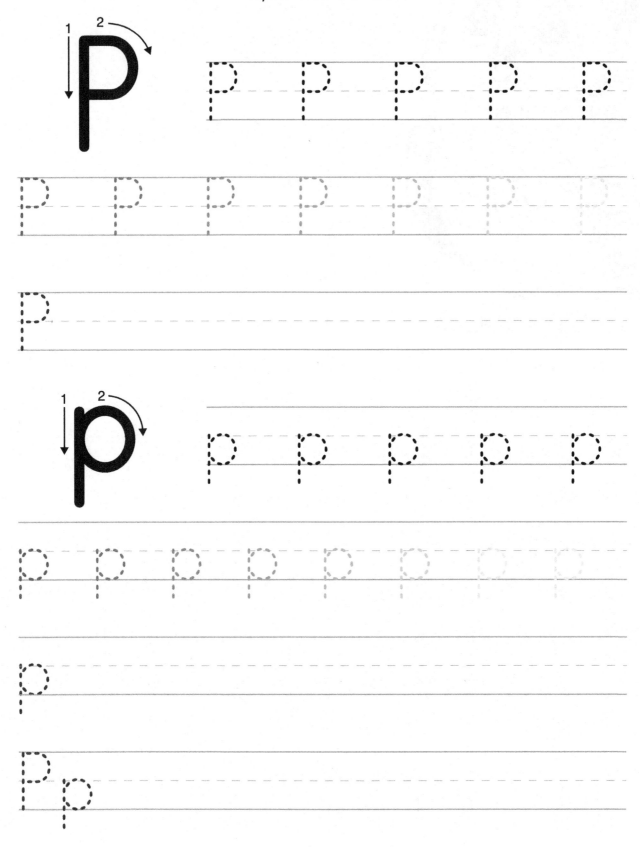

Jellyfish are 95% water.

Color in the flowers for Penny!

Trace the sentence:

Penny the pig spends

afternoons growing

colorful flowers in her

garden.

Ravens can solve puzzles.

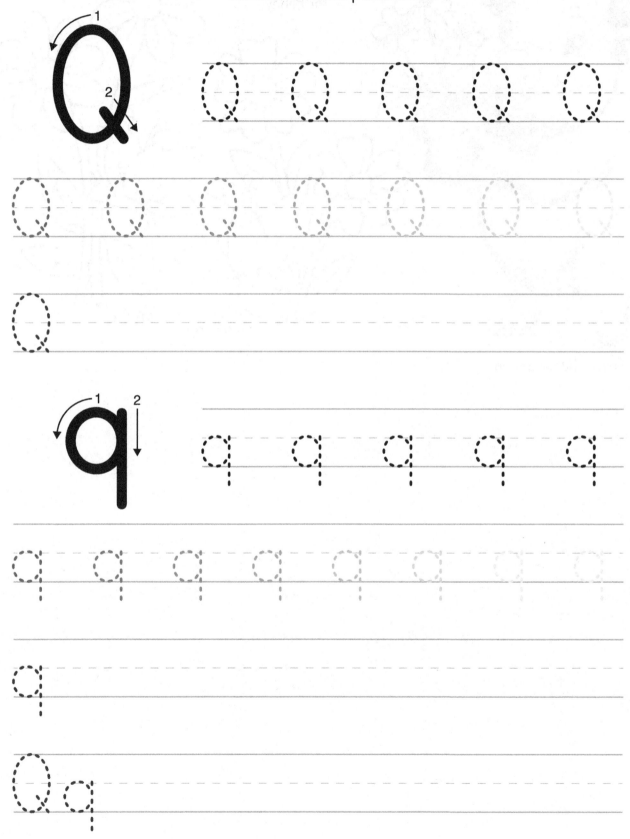

Draw an egg!

Trace the sentence:

Quincy the quail
carefully watches
over her tiny,
speckled egg.

Lobsters have blue blood.

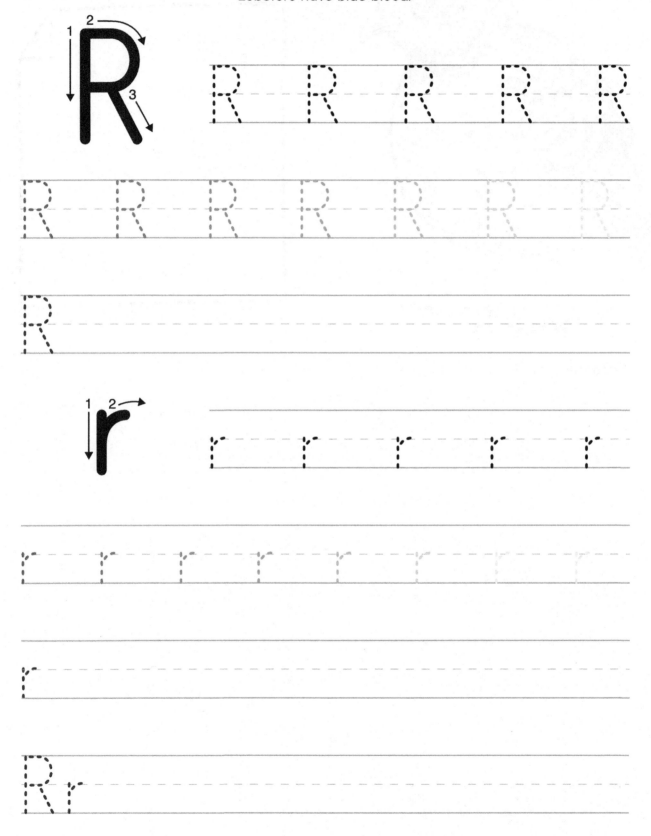

Help Ricky guide the ball through the
maze so it reaches the flagged hole.

41

Trace the sentence:

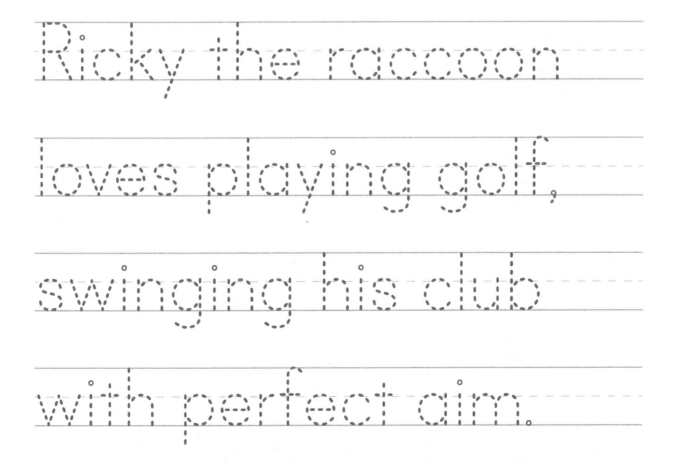

Ricky the raccoon

loves playing golf,

swinging his club

with perfect aim.

Koalas sleep up to 22 hours a day.

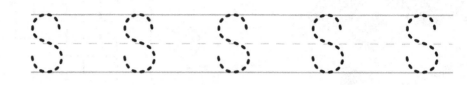

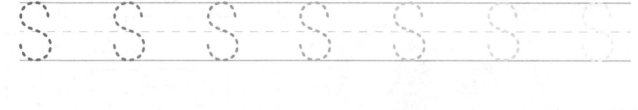

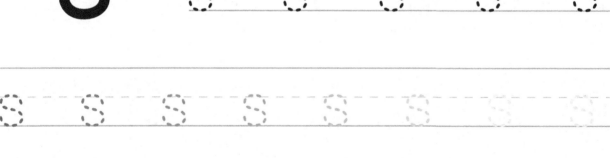

```
X X S D N E I R F A
P N N M E R U N O A
A U O T Z J D L S H
R F O K P E J Y T N
T S L C I S U M N U
Y E L J T C A K E U
A M A Y Z H C B S H
Y A B C A N D L E S
B G X G K B W Q R E
R M G N N K Z U P Z
```

Party   Cake   Balloons   Games   Friends
Fun   Presents   Candles   Music

Trace the sentence:

Sally the sheep is

in a hurry, racing to

make it on time to

the birthday party.

A kangaroo's tail is used for balance.

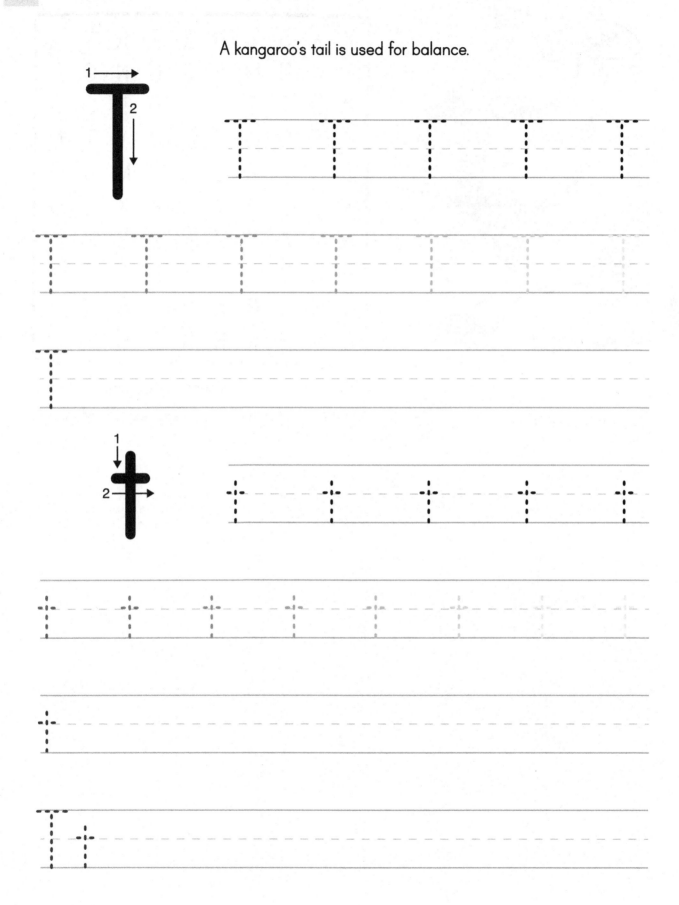

		3		1	
5	6		3	2	
	5	4	2		3
2		6	4	5	
	1	2		4	5
	4		1		

Fill in the sudoku puzzle so that every row across, every column down and every 2 by 3 box contains the numbers 1 to 6.

Trace the sentence:

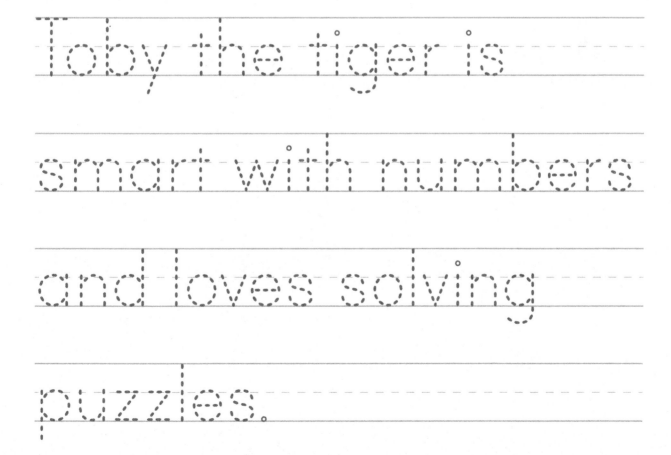

Toby the tiger is
smart with numbers
and loves solving
puzzles.

46

Frogs drink through their skin.

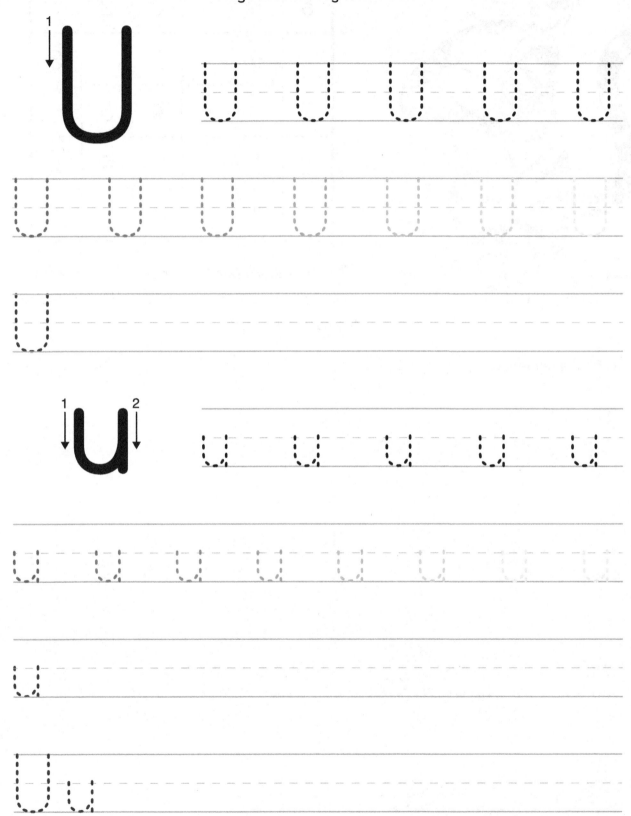

Color the image using the numbers below.

1 = Brown, 2 = Pink, 3 = Red, 4 = Blue

Trace the sentence:

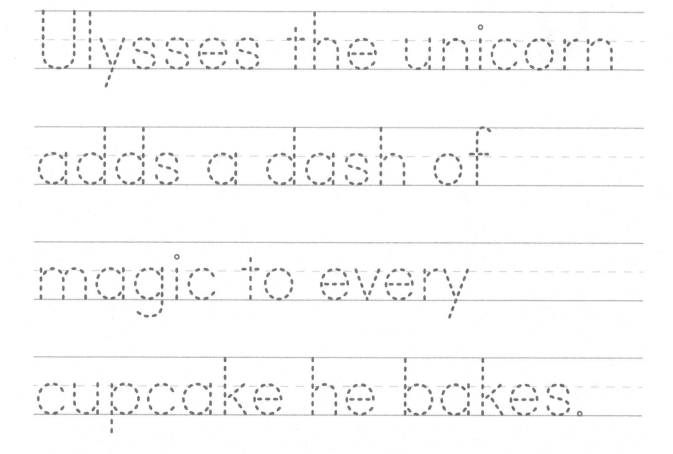

Ulysses the unicorn

adds a dash of

magic to every

cupcake he bakes.

Dolphins can recognize themselves in a mirror.

DID YOU KNOW?

Vultures are known as large **birds of prey,** but they typically feed on dead animals rather than hunting live ones.

They play a vital role in nature by **cleaning up dead animals** and preventing the spread of disease.

Some vultures can **soar for hours** without flapping their wings, riding on warm air currents called thermals.

Trace the sentence:

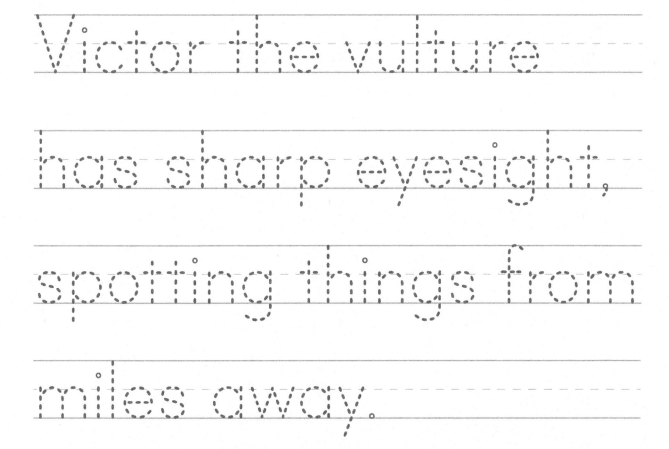

Victor the vulture has sharp eyesight, spotting things from miles away.

Crocodiles can swim up to 20 miles per hour.

Help Wesley create a new
colorful design for the T-shirt!

Trace the sentence:

Wesley the wolf
loves fashion and
wants to become a
designer someday.

Gorillas can catch human colds.

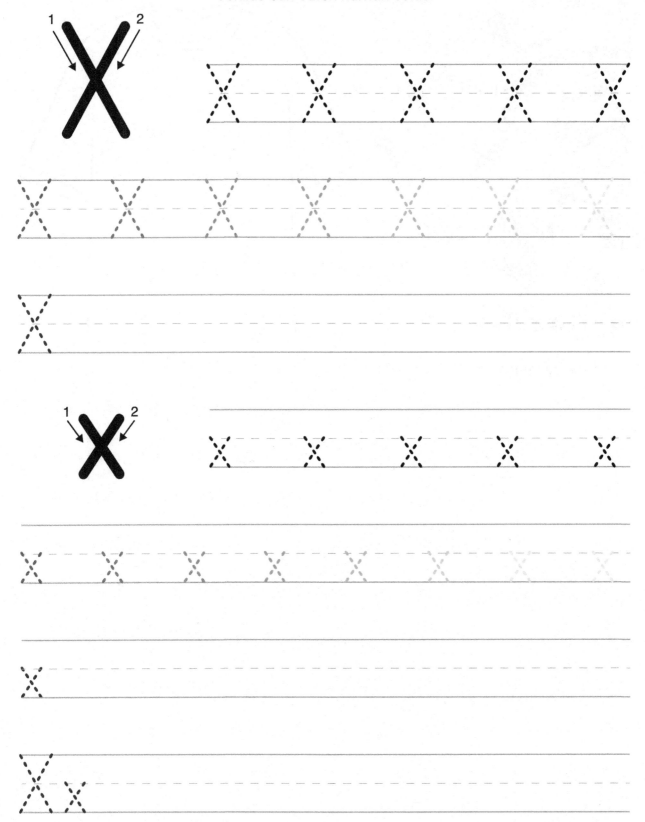

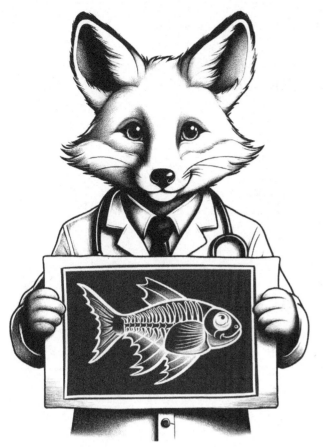

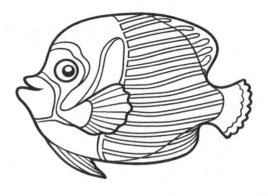

Trace the sentence:

Dr. Felix the fox carefully examines the fish's X-ray to check for any issues.

Cheetahs can't roar, but they can purr.

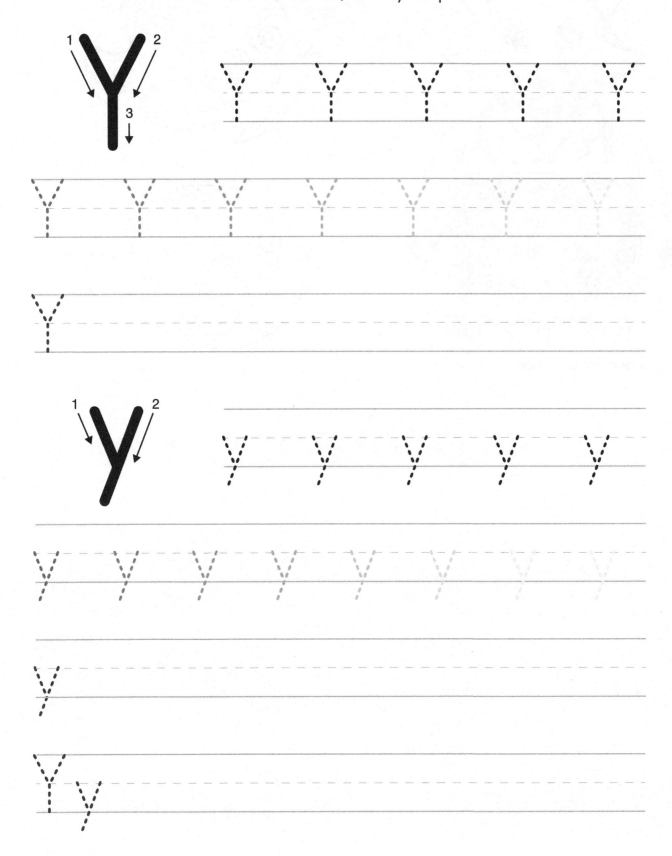

Draw in the missing pictures so that each row, column and 2x2 grid contains one and only one of each picture.

Trace the sentence:

Yago the yak cools

off with a big

serving of frozen

yogurt.

An ostrich's brain is smaller than its eye.

Ha!

Ha!

Ha!

Q: Why do zebras have stripes?
A: Because they don't want to be spotted.

Q: Which animals are the best at karate?
A: Zebras! They have so many black belts!

Q: Why is it so difficult to sell a toy zebra?
A: You can never find the barcode.

Trace the sentence:

Zane the zebra's sense of humor is so sharp, he laughs at his own jokes.

58

Jellyfish have no brains, hearts, or bones.

Some snakes can survive for months without food.

a b c d e f g

h i j k l m n

o p q r s t u

v w x y z

Cows can walk up stairs but not down.

Aa

Bb

Cc

Dd

Ee

Ff

Gg

Hh

Ii

Jj

An eagle's eyesight is eight times stronger than a human's.

Kk

Ll

Mm

Nn

Oo

Pp

Qq

Rr

Ss

Tt

Pigeons can be trained to deliver messages.

Uu

Vv

Ww

Xx

Yy

Zz

Oysters can change gender multiple times.

PART 2
Numbers

Armadillos can roll into a ball for protection.

Did you know that lemurs love eating figs? Help the lemur find the correct path to reach his favorite treat!

Parrots can live up to 80 years.

Camels can drink 40 gallons of water at once.

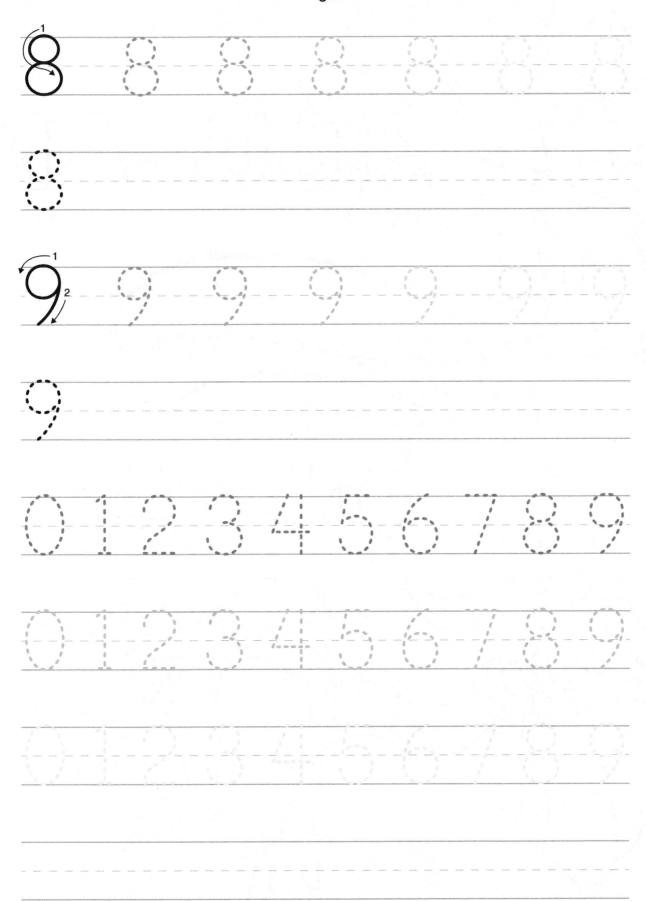

TOUCAN

Trace the numbers and repeat them in the empty space.

11	12	13	14	15
16	17	18	19	20
21	22	23	24	25
26	27	28	29	30
31	32	33	34	35
36	37	38	39	40
41	42	43	44	45
46	47	48	49	50
51	52	53	54	55

Squirrels plant thousands of trees each year by forgetting where they bury acorns.

56	57	58	59	60
61	62	63	64	65
66	67	68	69	70
71	72	73	74	75
76	77	78	79	80
81	82	83	84	85
86	87	88	89	90
91	92	93	94	95
96	97	98	99	100

Help the turtle find her way to the eggs. Don't forget to color them in!

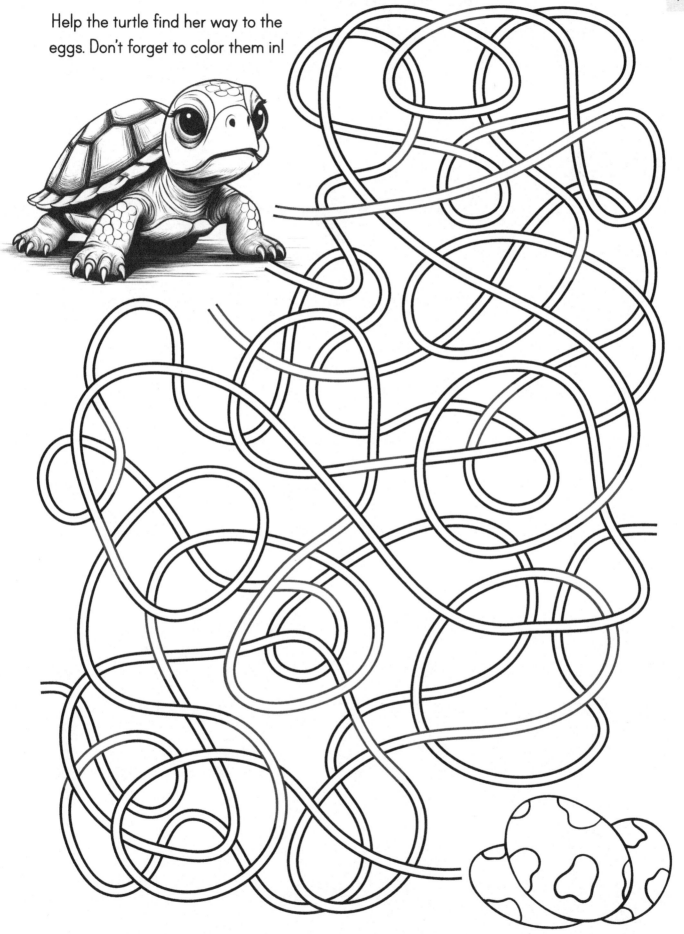

Trace the number word and write it.

Zero

One

Two

Three

Four

Five

Six

Seven

Eight

Nine

Ten

Eleven

Twelve

Thirteen

Fourteen

Fifteen

Sixteen

Seventeen

Eighteen

Nineteen

Twenty

Thirty

Forty

Fifty

Sixty

Seventy

Eighty

Ninety

Hundred

Thousand

PART 3
Sight Words

Trace the words.

after after after

again again again

an an an

any any any

as as as

ask ask ask

by by

could could could

every every every

fly fly fly

A blue whale's heart weighs as much as a car.

from from from

give give give

going going

had had had

has has has

her her her

him him him

his his his

Hyenas make a sound that resembles a laugh when communicating.

how how how

just just just

CHAMELEON

Crocodiles can live over 100 years.

know know know

let let let

live live live

may may may

old old old

once once once

open open open

over over over

put put put

round round round

Kangaroos carry their babies, called **joeys**, in their **pouches**.

Sloths move so slowly that algae grows on them.

some   some   some

stop   stop   stop

take   take   take

thank   thank   thank

them   them   them

then   then   then

think   think   think

walk   walk   walk

were   were   were

when   when   when

Connect the dots and color in the picture!

DOLPHIN

Trace the words and fill in the blanks with the proper word.

Before been always

because around best

DID YOU KNOW?

Owls are _____ hunting at night.

Dolphins swim _____ in groups for protection.

Penguins huddle _____ it helps them stay warm.

Camels have _____ used for transport for centuries.

_____ hibernation, bears eat a lot to store fat for the winter.

The cheetah is the _____ at running fast.

Giant panda babies are 900 times smaller in size than their mothers.

both both both

buy buy buy

call call call

cold cold cold

does does does

don't don't don't

fast fast fast

first first first

Octopuses hold onto prey with their strong suction cups.

five five five

found found found

Seahorse males carry the babies.

gave gave gave

goes goes goes

green green green

its its its

made made made

many many many

off off off

pull pull pull

read read read

right right right

Crows are highly intelligent and can use tools.

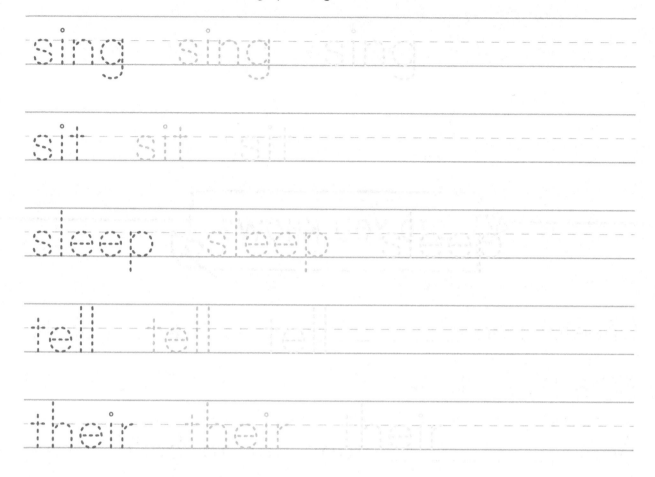

sing   sing   sing

sit   sit   sit

sleep   sleep   sleep

tell   tell   tell

their   their   their

Search and circle the hidden words!

T	E	L	L	N	C	O	T	A	O
P	S	N	X	R	I	G	H	T	F
C	L	I	W	M	A	N	Y	U	F
C	E	T	C	G	A	V	E	B	F
T	E	S	L	P	U	L	L	L	Q
H	P	S	O	E	N	M	S	G	G
E	N	I	M	A	D	E	F	R	G
I	W	T	A	U	C	E	C	E	O
R	E	A	D	S	I	N	G	E	E
E	N	X	C	C	R	C	M	N	S

- Gave
- Goes
- Green
- Its
- Made
- Many
- Off
- Pull
- Read
- Right
- Sing
- Sit
- Sleep
- Tell
- Their

DID YOU KNOW?

Lions use **their roar** to communicate over long distances.

Trace the words and fill in the blanks with the proper word.

wash which work

use very

DID YOU KNOW?

Cheetahs are _____ fast, running up to 60 miles per hour.

Ants _____ together to build large underground colonies.

Elephants use their trunks, _____ are very strong, to lift heavy objects.

Beavers _____ their teeth to cut down trees and build dams.

Otters love to play and _____ themselves in rivers.

or   or   or

these   these   these

those   those   those

upon   upon   upon

us   us   us

Sea otters hold hands
while they sleep to
avoid drifting apart.

why   why   why

wish   wish   wish

would   would   would

write   write   write

your   your   your

Help the hedgehog find his way to the sweet apple treat!

DID YOU KNOW?

Though **hedgehogs look cute**, these spiky mammals are **fierce predators** with a varied diet. They eat worms, slugs, beetles, and other small insects, and occasionally frogs, baby birds, snakes, eggs, and fruit.

about about about

better better better

bring bring bring

carry carry carry

clean clean clean

cut cut

Giraffes have to **spread their legs** wide to drink water.

done done done

draw draw draw

drink drink drink

fall fall fall

Giraffes have the same number of neck bones as humans.

far   far   far

full   full   full

got   got   got

grow   grow   grow

hold   hold   hold

hot   hot   hot

hurt   hurt   hurt

if   if   if

keep   keep   keep

kind   kind   kind

Color the picture!

JAGUAR

Cows have best friends.

laugh laugh laugh

light light light

long long long

much much much

myself myself myself

never never never

only only only

own own own

pick pick pick

shall shall shall

Cheetahs are the fastest land animals.

show   show   show

small   small   small

start   start   start

today   today   today

together   together   together

try   try   try

warm   warm   warm

SLOTH

Color the picture!

Sea otters have pockets under their arms for **storing food.**

Alligators can regrow their teeth.

Sea turtles have been
around for more than
100 million years.

Polar bears have black skin under their fur.

CERTIFICATE
OF COMPLETION

This Certificate is Proudly Presented to

For learning how to write in print

 # 1

Signature

Date

Thank you!

As a family-run, independent publisher, feedback
is essential for promoting our work. We would
greatly appreciate an honest review from you.

ZEFIRS PUBLISHING

zefirspublishing@gmail.com

Made in the USA
Coppell, TX
07 November 2024

39816298R00057